CONTROL YOUR ANGER

Control Your Anger

Apostle Dr. Victor Adewusi

Contents

Foreword		vii
Preface		ix
1	Anger is a Normal Emotion	1
2	What we Should Always Remember	5
3	Other Major Causes of Anger	9
4	How to Control Anger	12
5	What Causes Anger and Anger Problems?	16
6	Instances of Anger Displayed in the Bible	19
7	Is the Bible Very Categorial About Anger?	27
8	Forgiveness	32
9	The Role of Love	39
A Sinner's Prayer		45
About the Author		47

Copyright © 2022 by Aposle Dr. Victor Adewusi

All rights reserved. No part of this book may be used or reproduced by any means, graphics, electronic, or mechanical, including photocopying, recording, taping or by any information storage retrieval system without the author's written permission except in cases of brief quotations embodied in critical articles and reviews.

All scripture quotations are from the Holy Bible, New Living Translation, copyright © 1996, 2004, 2015 by Tyndale House Foundation. Used by permission of Tyndale House Publishers, Inc., Carol Stream, Illinois 60188. All rights reserved unless otherwise stated.

Scripture quotations marked NIV are taken from the Holy Bible, New International Version®, NIV® Copyright ©1973, 1978, 1984, 2011 by Biblica, Inc.® Used by permission. All rights reserved worldwide.

Scripture quotations marked NKJV are taken from the New King James Version®. Copyright © 1982 by Thomas Nelson. Used by permission. All rights reserved.

Author: Apostle Dr. Victor Adewusi

ISBN: 978-1-989099-03-2 (hardcover)
ISBN: 978-1-989099-11-7 (ebook)

First Printing, 2022

Foreword

I am most honoured to be doing this, especially considering I virtually learnt about taming my anger from the deceased author. As my biological father, I could say I have watched Apostle Adewusi pass on ways of pouring oil on troubled waters to all and sundry.

Apostle Adewusi was a counsellor amidst many, truly exceptional in his doings, not hypocritical and drew strength from his close relationship with God and his bible.

Many years ago, as a young man, I erred and was unruly to my father. I expected severe reproach. Rather than that, some bible verses were shared and discussed like mates. I was shocked because I knew he exercised restraints by internalising before reacting. It made a whole lot of difference for me; till this day, before reacting, I try to countdown.

Let me also point out that I am a Teacher in one of the European countries where earlier, it was easy to be angered by the way people reacted to me initially. Due to the teachings and guidance of my father, bible verses teaching on combating hatred with love and compassion, steps and principles in this book, I became slower to volatile anger. I am perceived as a calm and likeable teacher and leader in my society.

With almost 8 billion people and counting, 58.53 people per square kilometer, it's appropriate to say that finding a way to mingle peacefully while standing up for oneself is paramount.

It is a beautiful time to live; however, the fight for resources between nations, ego and power tussles between leaders, family squabbles at the Christmas table, school killings, terrorism, and spiritual battles, just to name a few, lead to monsters and not men. This book effectively provides readers and me with a constant reminder not to allow anger to dehumanize us while providing apt biblical backing to soothe the angered mind.

There are thousands of people that have benefited from the immense wisdom of the author. He acted and lived as described in the book, always slow to anger and willing to listen.

As the author mentioned, love is endearing while anger alienates you. Pent-up anger kills.

Chiding from the perspective of love and receiving criticism with maturity and wisdom.

I do wholeheartedly recommend getting a copy of this book for all those in your circle of interest.

Joseph Adewusi

Preface

I give God all the glory for giving me the ability to finally break the jinx of sitting down to fulfill one of my long-term passions in life, which is to become an accomplished authour.

Although I've made several attempts to do what I am doing now, several factors have always hindered me from crossing the hurdle; but to God alone be all the glory and adoration.

From the very tender age of six, I began to vividly witness severe fighting and dangerous exchange of broken bottle blows, knives, and cudgels during fisticuffs. On most occasions, it was among a particular couple with whom we lived in the same house on Lagos Island in Nigeria.

The fighting usually lasted more than 2-3 hours, which almost always unavoidably attracted outsiders to the ugly scene. They would harm each other; and, in most instances, would be rushed to the hospital for treatment. Broken bottles would litter the entire apartment, while television sets, radios, and many other household decors would usually be destroyed in the crossfire. However, what was baffling to me, as young as I was, was that they usually put up the display and show of shame almost every month or at most twice, within every three months. They were adults in their late forties, but the wife was older than the husband; their tribes differ.

Since that period of my life, which spanned over six decades ago, I began to nurture the idea of writing a book on "anger." I saw acrimony at its peak and anger in an awful form. Not only that, our neighbourhood contained different types of street urchins and dangerous elements, including boys and girls who indulged in the smoking of weed (cannabis) and other negatively intoxicating consumables. The resultant effects and endpoints were uncontrollable fights, quarrels, and the exchange of dangerous weapons, which usually occurred during the daytime.

Today, however, we are more exposed to greater end rage than ever before. Domestic violence, spousal abuse, gang wars, road rage and personal assault are growing to disturbing levels. Both in print and electronic, the media cannot even cover the reportage in full.

The Hebrew word for "anger" comes from the words "face" and "nostrils." And whoever might have faced a truly angry person would understand why. It distorts our facial appearance whenever anger builds up, an outward manifestation of a very fiery volcano within us! Anger, if unchecked, can eat away at the heart and affect a person's character, no matter how highly placed the individual may be.

Yet, anger is not always destructive, as we shall soon discover from the pages of this book. Anger, in its healthy form, if properly controlled and expressed, can motivate us to work for a positive change. Anger, when checked, is like a refiner's fire that tempers steel to make it stronger; however, if it remains unchecked, it could be as destructive as the wildfires that occasionally flare up in the hillside chaparral of southern California, USA.

I encourage you to read and go through each line of this book with undivided attention and read it as many times as possible. Please endeavour to apply the principles as often as practicably possible as you do so.

It is a reader's favourite. It is helpful for both the young and the elderly: recommended for Sunday school teachers, the clergy, preachers, parents, guardians, husbands, wives, lovers, children, students and organizers of seminars and conferences.

1

Anger is a Normal Emotion

Anger is a normal emotion that everyone experiences from time to time. However, if one sees that anger turns to aggression or outbursts, one should find other healthy ways to deal with it.

Anger is a strong passion or emotion of displeasure, especially antagonism, excited by a sense of injury or insult. Although we usually think of anger as an emotion, it is, in reality, a cluster of emotions that involve the body, the mind, the will and our spiritual life.

On most occasions, becoming angry is not planned but an automatic reaction to unavoidable situations, circumstances, instances or experiences in life that causes us irritation, frustration, physical pain or spiritual displeasure. On the other hand, anger could be a deliberate action or a reaction to sudden or piled-up issues, matters or events.

It could occur due to feelings of disappointment, hurt, rejection, embarrassment or shame. The list is quite endless where it can happen: between spouses, parents and their children, bosses and their employees, amongst colleagues, pastors against their congregation or even amongst neighbours. However, it is instructive to state that the first recorded incident of anger in the Bible arose between Cain and Abel, according to Genesis 4:3-8. It was due to envy and jealousy, for verse 8 says, *"Now Cain said to his brother Abel, let us go out to the field. And while they were in the field, Cain attacked his brother Abel and killed him."*

Anger could also be regarded as the uncontrolled fits of unbridled emotions resulting from the absence of love, affection and care. On most occasions, anger occurs when we find it extremely difficult to control our temper, just like Cain mentioned above. Anger has no gender, nor is it measured by age, status, or anyone's position in society.

In life, I have discovered that blame-shifting could easily lead to the exchange of harsh and hot words, which could ultimately blow up emotions of fits, anger and sometimes the exchange of fisticuffs. In Genesis 3:12-13 (NIV), Adam and Eve tried to shift blame. Adam said to Eve, *"The woman you put here with me - she gave me some fruit from the tree, and I ate it."* Then the Lord said to Eve, *"What is this that you have done? The woman said, "The serpent deceived me, and I ate it."* Some people even try to blame God, as recorded in Proverbs 19:3 (NIV), *"A person's own folly leads to their ruin, yet their heart rages against the Lord."* We must never judge others while we fail to acknowledge our own sin, according to Matthew 7:1-5 (NIV), which says, *"Do not judge, or you too will be judged. For in the same way you judge others, you will be judged, and with the measure you use, it will be measured to you. Why do you look at the speck of sawdust in your brother's eye and pay no attention to the plank in your eye? You hypocrite, first take the plank out of your own eye, and then you will see clearly to remove the speck from your brother's eye."*

If we are to rid our lives of anger, we should avoid the tripod of bitterness, hate and resentment as much as possible. Ephesians 4:31-32 (NIV) says, *"Get rid of all bitterness, rage and anger, brawling and slander, along with every form of malice. Be kind and compassionate to one another, forgiving each other, just as in Christ God forgave you."* Galatians 5:15 (NIV) says, *"If you bite and devour each other, watch out or you will be destroyed by each other."* We should, therefore, let no bitterness grow; Hebrews 12:15 (NIV), *"See to it that no one falls short of the grace of God and that no bitter root grows up to cause trouble and defile many."* Remember what Joseph's brothers did by allowing bitterness to grow into hatred and murder in their hearts simply because of the dream he had and shared with his siblings about his future. Therefore, we must avoid and eschew hatred because God forbids it; Leviticus 19:16-17 (NIV), *"Do not go about spreading slander among your people. Do not do anything that endangers your neighbor's life. I am the Lord. Do not hate a fellow Israelite in your heart. Rebuke your neighbour frankly so that you will not share in their guilt."*

The following scriptures encourage us that:

1. **Hatred is murder:** I John 3:11-20 & I John 3:15 (NIV) explicitly reiterates that *"Anyone who hates a brother or sister is a murderer"* (remember Cain to Abel), *"and you know that no murderer has eternal life residing in him."*
2. **Someone who hates lives in darkness:** I John 2:9-11
3. **Jesus encourages us NOT to hate our enemies but to LOVE and pray for them:** Matthew 5:43-48
4. **Hatred stirs up dissension:** Proverbs 10:12.
5. **We should be slow to anger:** Proverbs 14:16-17, *"A wise man fears the Lord and shuns evil, but a fool is hotheaded and reckless. A quick tempered man does foolish things and a crafty man is hated."*
6. **Hot words stir up strife:** Proverbs 15:1, *"A gentle answer turns away wrath, but a harsh word stirs up anger."*

Whenever provoked, we must control ourselves because fits of rage belong to our sinful nature, which is the way of sin.

Proverbs 25:28 - *"Like a city whose walls are broken down is a man who lacks self control."*

Proverbs 29:22 - *"An angry man stirs up dissension, and a hot tempered one commits many sins."*

Proverbs 19:11 - *"Sensible people control their temper; they earn respect by overlooking wrongs."*

2

What we Should Always Remember

Although under provocation, it might not be that easy to control ourselves quickly, we should nonetheless endeavour to remember that love covers a multitude of sins and overlooks many offences.

Proverbs 12:16 - *"A fool shows his annoyance at once, but a prudent man overlooks an insult."*

Proverbs 17:9 - *"He who covers an offence promotes love, but whoever repeats the matter separates close friends."*

According to **Ephesians 4:26**, the Bible says, *"In your anger, do not sin; do not let the sun go down while you are still angry."*

We must constantly remember that anger can be expressed in a positive manner, especially when a person's intent is to save a falling or bad situation. Such examples of this are when we "shout" at someone to show or express our concern for that person or "to sit up" and "adjust" or refrain from "slowing down" in taking quick and prompt remedial steps. Anger is not in itself sinful, as shown below:

1. God expressed anger towards wickedness in **Psalm 7:11**.
2. Jesus expressed anger towards the Pharisees in **Mark 3:5**.
3. Jesus demonstrated his anger with Isreal in **2 Kings 17**.
4. The Lord demonstrated His anger towards Solomon in **I Kings 11:9**. Mark 10:42-44 highlights that world leaders are often pushy and domineering; however, we must lead with humility and love as Christians. Matthew 5:38-41, *"Ye have heard that an eye for an eye, and a tooth for a tooth; but I say to you that ye resist not evil but whosoever shall smite thee on thy right cheek, the him the other also. And if any man will sue thee at the law, and take away thy coat, let him have thy clothe also. And whosoever shall compel thee to go a mile, go with him further."*
5. **Ecclesiastes 7:9** - *"Be not hasty in thy spirit to be angry for anger rests in the bosom of fools."*
6. **Psalm 37:8** - *"Cease from anger and forsake wrath; fret not thyself in any wise to do evil."*

Some of the things we should always be conscious of concerning anger are discussed more in-depth hereunder. If we could exercise patience, we may sometimes realize that what makes us angry could become something that we could benefit from. In Job 19:13-21, Job lost everything, and everybody deserted him during his trial by the devil. Still, God returned everything to him because he knew his Redeemer Liveth. Similarly, in Psalm 38:10-11, even though King David was lonely and afflicted, and felt separated from his loved ones, he was forced to draw closer to God.

Instead of becoming angry, we should always realize that we have a friend in Jesus who is always closer to us than any best friend, according to Proverbs 18:24. So, instead of getting angry whenever people disappoint, we must always remember how in Luke 23:49, the friends of Jesus Christ stood afar on the day that He died on the cross. This should give us consolation that if it could happen to Jesus Christ, then it could happen to anybody. Listen to what that portion says, *"And all His acquaintances, and the women that followed Him from Galilee, stood afar off, beholding these things."*

Many victims of anger and bitterness are usually unable to control their pride and selfishness according to Proverbs 21:24, *"Proud and haughty scorner is his Name who dealeth in proud wrath."*

As much as we can, we should do everything humanly possible to control our temper so that it does not cause more problems for us, as seen in the case of Moses. According to Numbers 20:7-12, God told him to strike the rock once, but in anger, he did so twice, which annoyed God. Psalm 106:32-33 also illustrates Moses' anger on display through his use of rash words. This anger and disobedience prevented him from entering the Promised Land.

Instead of getting annoyed or fueling anger, we should try our best to be like Abigail in I Samuel 25:1-35. She wisely pacified her husband, King David, when he wanted to kill the husband of Bathsheba. David was forced to thank and appreciate Abigail openly by saying, *"Blessed be the Lord God of Israel who sent you this day to meet me! And blessed be thy advice, and blessed be thou which has kept me this day from coming to shed blood, and from avenging myself with my own hand."* How many of us can do that? Instead, many would preferably attack their father's "perceived enemy" in support, rather than calming frayed nerves.

As Believers, we must strive to be in the spirit at all times. Why? Frustration could be the reason for our anger, and if we are frustrated, we must ask God to lead us out of it instead of looking for whom we could "purge' our rage on. And that frustration could be due to a lack of faith and trust in the Lord, as exemplified below:

1. **Psalm 119:165** - *"Great peace have they which love thy law, and nothing shall offend them."*
2. **Romans 8:25** - *"But if we hope for that which we see not, then with patience, we wait for it."*
3. **Philippians 4:6-7** - *"Be anxious for nothing, but in everything by prayer and supplication with thanksgiving, let your requests be made known unto God. And the peace of God, which passeth all understanding, shall keep your hearts and minds through Christ Jesus."*
4. **Proverbs 13:12** - Hear what the scripture says, *"God's delays are not always denials, but when the desire cometh, it is a tree of life."* This scripture must constantly be in our hearts because some people become angry, frustrated, disappointed and discouraged. After all, God has "not answered their prayer requests on time."
5. **Proverbs 21:30** - If the Lord does not want something done, no matter how "good or beautiful" your ideas and plans are, they will not work. And according to Ecclesiastes 3:1-8, to everything, there is a season and a time to every purpose under heaven.
6. **Psalm 37:4-5** - Strongly says, If you put God first and trust Him, He will help to put things to work out. *"Delight thyself also in the Lord, and He shall give thee the desires of thine heart. Commit thy ways unto the Lord, trust also in Him, and He shall bring it to pass."*

Thus, the majority of us become angry due to "undue delay" by God in our sight instead of confessing what the Book of Psalms 44:6 says, *"I will not trust in my bow, neither shall my sword save me."* Hear what John 15:5 says, *"I am the Vine, ye are the branches. He that abideth in Me, and I in him, the same bringeth forth much fruit, for without Me, ye can do nothing."*

3

Other Major Causes of Anger

No one prays for unforeseen circumstances or situations, but no matter what losses we may suffer, we must never become unduly angry because Jesus Christ is always there for us.

Psalm 27:10 (NKJV) - *"When my father and my mother forsake me, Then the Lord will take care of me."*

Psalm 142:4-5 - *"I looked on my right and my left hand, and behold, no man would know me; refuge failed me, and no man cared for my soul. I cried unto thee, O Lord, I said Thou art my refuge and my portion in the land of the Living."*

Isaiah 54:10 - *"For the mountains shall depart, And the hills be removed," Says the Lord, but my kindness shall not depart from thee; neither shall the covenant of peace be removed, saith the Lord that hath mercy on thee."*

Always bear in mind that, instead of becoming annoyed or irritated due to one thing or the other, **John 14:18** says, *"Jesus Christ will not leave you comfortless; I will come to you."* This scripture should console us at all times.

Some people become annoyed because they cannot tolerate others! Are you surprised? The Bible is very emphatic about it:

1. **I Corinthians 3:1-5** - Being intolerant of the differences of others can reveal a lack of maturity. *"And I, brethren, could not speak unto you as unto spiritual, but as unto carnal, even as babes in Christ. I have fed you with milk........even as the Lord gave to every man?"* This is why we are admonished to follow peace with all men and holiness, without which no man shall see the Lord.
2. **Luke 17:4** - *"And if he trespasses against thee seven times in a day, and seven times in a day, turn again to thee, saying, I repent, thou shall forgive him."*
3. **Romans 14:1** - We are encouraged to tolerate one another's weaknesses except when it comes to speaking doubt and sowing discord.
4. **Romans 15:2** - We that are strong ought to bear the infirmities of the weak and not to please ourselves.
5. **Galatians 6:1** - *"Brethren, if a man be overtaken in a fault, ye which are spiritual should restore such one in the spirit of meekness, considering thyself lest thou also be tempted."*

Instead of being relaxed, many persons are angered as a result of undue worry, which can solve no issue according to Psalm 127: 1-2, which says that except the Lord built the house, they labour in vain who built it.

Matthew 6:25-34 encourages us not to worry about the future or about His faithfulness to supply our daily needs: *"Behold the fowls of the air, for they sow not, neither do they reap nor gather unto barns; yet your heavenly Father feeds them. Are you not of more value than they?"*

Numbers 13:28-33 - The devil uses worry, fear, and by extension, anger to exaggerate our troubles if our faith is not very strong in the Lord.

Psalm 37:1 - *"Fret not, thyself because of evildoers, neither be thou envious against the workers of iniquity."* This scripture tells us that comparing ourselves with unbelievers or the ungodly ones could warrant undue envy and untold anger, which we must avoid as much as possible.

That is why God admonishes us in Psalm 55:22 to cast our burdens and worries on Him instead of getting annoyed. *"Cast thy burden upon the Lord, and He shall sustain thee. He shall never suffer the righteous to be moved."* Same with Matthew 11:28-30, *"Come unto Me, all ye that labour and are heavy laden, and I will give you rest. Take my yoke upon you, and lean on Me.....for my yoke is easy, and My burden is light."*

Whenever we are pressured to become angry because of situations in our lives that seem insurmountable, let us always take solace in what Apostle Paul wrote to the people in 2 Corinthians 4:8-9, *"We are pressured on every side but not crushed; perplexed, but not in despair; persecuted but not abandoned, struck down but not destroyed."* Is that not reassuring and powerful, instead of being downcast and worried? Paul also said in the same 2 Corinthians 11:23-28 that *"I have worked much harder, been in prison more frequently, been flogged more severally and been exposed to death again and again....Besides everything else, I face daily the pressure of my concern for all the Churches."*

4

How to Control Anger

Anger management is important for helping someone avoid saying or doing something they may regret. Thus, before anger escalates, one can use specific strategies to control anger.

According to the title of this book, we can put our anger under effective control by any or a combination of the following methods:

1. Always think before you speak. In the heat of the moment, it is easy to say something one will regret later. It is thus advisable to take a few moments to collect one's thoughts before saying anything and allow others involved in the situation to do the same. We must realize that keeping one's temper in control can be challenging.
2. Proceed to express anger once calm. As soon as one has started to think clearly, they can now express their feelings in an assertive but non-confrontational manner. State concerns and emotions clearly and specifically, without hurting others or trying to control them.
3. Physical activity can help to reduce the stress that can cause someone to become angry. Once one feels that his anger is on the upward trend, it is advisable to move away from the source

and open up after some time of doing other enjoyable physical activities.
4. Endeavour to identify immediate possible solutions. Hence, instead of focusing on what made you worried or disturbed, work on resolving the issue at hand. Always remind yourself that anger would not fix anything and might only worsen the situation on the ground.
5. Attempt to not hold a grudge against anybody among the crowd. This is where forgiveness comes in. Why? It is a powerful tool, so much so that an entire chapter of this book has been dedicated to it. If we allow anger and other negative feelings to crowd our positive feelings, one might find himself swallowed up by his own bitterness or an extreme sense of injustice. However, if we can forgive someone who annoyed us, we can both learn from the situation and strengthen the relationship.
6. Skillfully use a great sense of humour to release tension. Using humour to deal with what is making you angry would diffuse any unrealistic expectations one has for how things should go and essentially help you to lighten up. Try to avoid sarcasm, as it can hurt feelings and make things worse.
7. Do not be shy, and know when to seek help. Learning to control anger is a very big challenge at times for most people. It is therefore desirable to seek help whenever one's anger seems to be getting out of control or is causing someone to do terrible things that they could regret or hurt those around you.
8. It is advisable to practice deep breathing exercises whenever temper seems to be on the increase, or begin to repeat a calming word or phrases such as God, help me, or Lord, take control, and Take it easy (mention your Name, e.g. Take it, Beckley)
9. Since our breathing becomes shallower and speeds up as we grow angry, it is greatly advisable to quickly reverse that trend and the anger by deliberately slowing down the pace, though it might not be easy under high temper. Thus, take deep breaths from the nose and exhale them out of the mouth for several moments.

10. Engage in deliberate stretches, either of the neck or of the shoulders, because they help to control the body and harness emotions. And this does not warrant any big or major equipment.
11. Begin to gently move away into a quiet environment and close your eyes after finding a comfortable place to sit down or relax your back. Gradually imagine yourself trying to calm some angered parties down.
12. Stop talking as soon as you notice that your temper is flaring. This way, you will be forced to avoid uttering any angry words that could aggravate the temper of others. Pretend as if your lips have been glued together. This moment without speaking will create an opportunity to rearrange your thought process.
13. Try to take any realistic and reasonable action, such as doing something good for someone else. Pour your energy and emotions into something that is healthy and productive.
14. Prevent an outburst by rehearsing what you are going to say or how you are going to approach the issue in the future. This rehearsal period also gives you enough time to role play several possible solutions.
15. Look out for, and talk to a trusted and more mature person or friend who can possibly provide a new perspective to the issues that have been disturbing you.
16. Have you ever tried to laugh under any serious provocation? One should, therefore, diffuse his anger by looking for ways to laugh, whether by watching hilarious movies or listening to interesting music.
17. Ponder on the great and amazing things that God has done in your life.
18. Express your anger now but try to avoid outbursts because it solves no problem but tends to aggravate it. Mature dialogue can help to reduce stress and ease one's anger as well as prevent future problems.
19. Identify the emotions if you want to drastically deal with sadness and anger in the following manner:

- **Be aware of how you feel; thus, whenever you have a negative emotion, such as anger, try to name what you are feeling.**
- **Do not hide how you feel from yourself, be very frank.**
- **Know why you feel the way you do.**
- **Do not blame anybody.**
- **Accept all of your emotions as natural and understandable.**

At this juncture, please permit me to state categorically that everyone has experienced anger, including me, your Author, as nobody is immune to it. Our level of handling or dealing with it, however, differs tremendously. The intensity of one's anger can range from profound annoyance to extreme rage. It is normal and quite healthy to feel angry from time to time in response to certain situations. However, people experience uncontrollable anger that often escalates, especially when the provocation is minor. In this case, anger is not a normal emotion but a major issue.

5

What Causes Anger and Anger Problems?

The issue of anger is a very exhaustive topic and can actually not be thoroughly dealt with it in one swell swoop. That is why I still want to shed more light on the causes and likely symptoms. Some common anger triggers include:

1. **Personal problems such as missing promotions at work or relationship difficulties**
2. **Problem caused by an external force (person, event, situation, etc.) - an event or a situation like bad traffic or getting involved in an accident, alone or along with others**
3. **Memories of a traumatic or enraging event. However, in other cases, anger problems may be caused by early trauma or events in a person's life that have shaped their personality.**
4. **Hormonal changes can also cause anger, as can occur in certain mental disorders or women's menstrual circles.**

Possible Symptoms

Some signs that one's anger is not normal could include any of or a combination of these:

1. **Anger that affects your relationships and social life**
2. **Staying away from certain situations because one is anxious or depressed about angry outbursts**
3. **Feeling compelled to do or doing violent or impulsive things because you feel angry, such as driving recklessly or destroying things**
4. **A glaring inability to control one's temper**
5. **Threatening violence to people or their property**
6. **Being physically violent whenever one is angry**
7. **Arguing with others often and getting angrier in the process**
8. **Constantly feeling impatient, irritated and hostile**
9. **Constant negative thinking and focusing on negative experiences**
10. **Feeling that you have to hide or hold your anger under control by force or through the support of other people**

Many people use anger to motivate them to do something positive. But if it is not managed properly, anger can have negative health effects. Expressing anger inappropriately or keeping anger pent up can aggravate chronic pain or lead to concerns like sleep and/or digestive disorders.

It is very pertinent to mention some common negative effects of anger, and after going through them, we should endeavour to identify our own weak points and begin to address them. Some of the short and long term health problems that have been linked to unmanaged anger include:

1. **Headache or stomach ache**
2. **Digestion problems, such as abdominal pains**
3. **Insomnia (inability to sleep soundly)**
4. **Increased anxiety**
5. **Depression**
6. **High blood pressure**
7. **Skin problems, such as eczema**
8. **Heart attack**
9. **Dwindling memory**
10. **Loss of creativity**
11. **Weakened concentration**
12. **Accusatory thoughts**
13. **Impaired immune system**
14. **Dizziness**

The list is not exhaustive; there are only three (3) general ways of expressing anger, which are:

1. **Aggressive**
2. **Passive**
3. **Assertive**

6

Instances of Anger Displayed in the Bible

Acts 19:28 - When they heard this and were filled with rage, they began to cry out, saying *"Great is Artemis of the Ephesians."*

Acts 17:16 - *"Now while Paul was waiting for them at Athens, his spirit was being provoked within him as he was observing the city full of idols."*

Matthew 26:8 - *"But the Disciples were indignant when they saw this, and said, 'Why this waste?'"*

Matthew 22:7 - *"But the King was enraged and he sent his Armies and destroyed those murderers and set their city on fire."*

Matthew 2:16 - *"Then when Herod saw that he had been tricked by the Magi, he became very enraged, and sent and slew all the male children who were in Bethlehem, and all its vicinity, from two years old and under, according to the time which he had determined from the Magi."*

Daniel 2:12 - *"Because of this, the King became indignant and very furious and gave orders to destroy all the wise men of Babylon."*

Jonah 4:1 - *"But it greatly displeased Jonah and he became angry."*

Jonah 4:4 - *The Lord said, "Do you have good reasons to be angry?"*

Nehemiah 4:7 - *"Now when Sanballat, Tobiah the Arabs, the Ammonites and the Ashdodites heard that the repair of Jerusalem went on, and that the breaches began to be closed, they were very angry."*

Daniel 3:13 - *"Then Nebuchadnezzar in rage and anger gave orders to bring Shadrach, Meshach and Abednego, then these Men were brought to the King."*

2 Kings 5:11-12 - *"But Naaman was furious and went away and said "Behold, I thought he will surely come out to me and stand and call on the Name of the Lord his God, and wave his hands over the place and cure the leper. 12. "Are not Abana and Pharpar, the rulers of Damascus, better than all the waters of Israel? Could I not wash in them and be clean? So he turned and went away in a rage."*

I Kings 21:4 - *"So Ahab came into his house sullen and vexed because of the word which Naboth the Jezreelite had spoken to him; for he said "I will not give you the inheritance of my fathers." And he lay down on his bed, turned away his face and ate no food."*

2 Samuel 13:21 - *"Now when King David heard of all these matters, he was very angry."*

I Samuel 11:6 - *"Then the Spirit of God came upon Saul mightily when he heard these words, and he became angry."*

Genesis 4:5-6 - *"But for Cain and his offering He had no regard. So Cain became very angry and his countenance fell. Then the Lord said to Cain, "Why are you angry? And why has your countenance fallen?"*

Exodus 17 - *"God told Moses to strike the rock with his staff but he struck the waters of the Nile river; God was angry."*

Numbers 20:10-13 - Moses and Aaron gathered the assembly of Israel before the rock at Meribah where God told him to speak to the rock to yield water, but he struck it twice and God was annoyed.

In addition to the foregoing, let us examine some of the Golden verses that I have referred to earlier, and discuss how we can overcome this cankerworm that has tended to wreck the lives of many personalities across the globe, and in the Bible.

Remember that every day of our life, there is a possibility to encounter many situations that can cause us to experience immediate emotional reactions. Feeling angry is a natural human response, and on most occasions, these feelings can be absolutely justified. However, one of the major ways that can help us to assuage our anger is to committedly read Bible verses about anger, as this helps us to deal with, and process this emotion.

Knowing what the Bible says about anger cannot only make us feel better and move away from anger to a more productive and positive emotion but can also equally help us to feel better and regain control over what is often a quick and better feeling.

Psalm 37:8 - *"Don't give into worry or anger; it only leads to trouble."* Whenever we act based on our negative emotions, we might make the wrong decisions. Hence we should take time to calm down before doing anything.

Proverbs 29:22 - *"People with quick tempers cause a lot of quarrelling and trouble."* Whenever someone is angry, they might offload their emotions on other people in one form or the other and cause problems or fights. We must try to stay away from those types of people.

Ecclesiastes 7:9 - *"Keep your temper under control; it is foolish to harbour a grudge."* Some situations can make us react angrily, and that is not bad, but we must not harbour anger and hold grudges because it is pointless and quite exhausting.

Proverbs 15:1 - *"A soft answer turns away wrath but a harsh word stirs up anger."* Whenever someone who is angry confronts us, we should try not to fight with them. We should try to talk to them calmly because it will help calm them down and make their anger dissipate.

Ephesians 4:26 - *"If you become angry, do not let your anger lead you to sin, and do not stay angry all day."* Whenever we are angry, we could unavoidably do something we might regret later or act in a way that could hurt those that are around us. We should wait until the anger dissipates before making a decision or taking any action.

Proverbs 14:17 - *"People with a hot temper do foolish things but wiser people remain calm."* Since anger is a normal response to some situations, it is how we respond to them that makes us or tells people who we are.

Matthew 5:22 - *"But I promise you that if you are angry with someone, you will have to stand trial. If you call someone a fool, you will be taken to court. And if you say that someone is worthless, you will be in danger of the fires of hell." We must always bear it in mind that all actions have consequences, especially if we act out of anger and pettiness.

Ephesians 4:31 - *"Get rid of all bitterness, passion and anger. No more shouting or insults, no more hateful feelings or acts of sort."* An angry person often pushes those around them away. When confronted with a situation that makes you angry, choose to remain calm and talk things out rather than fighting with the other party.

2 Timothy 2:23-25 - *"But keep away from foolish and ignorant arguments; you know that they end up in quarrels. As the Lord's servants, you must not quarrel. You must be kind towards all, a good and patient teacher, who is gentle as you correct your opponents, for it may be that God will give them the opportunity to repent, and come to know the truth."*

Whenever we surround ourselves with other people, we can pick up some of their behavioural attributes, which include their negative reactions to situations. Endeavour to stay away from those who pick fights over everything because it goes against the wishes and expectations of God.

Proverbs 14:29 - *"Those who control their anger have great understanding; those who have a hasty temper will make mistakes."* This implies that we only have great power when we are able to control our emotions and have patience, unlike those who allow their anger to control them.

Romans 12:21 - *"Don't let evil get the best of you, but conquer evil by doing good."* Always choose to do good rather than acting on your negative emotions.

James 1:19-20 - *"My dear Brothers and Sisters, take note of this; everyone should be quick to listen, slow to speak and slow to become angry, because human anger does not produce the righteousness that God desires."* We must keep our faith in God and trust that He will guide us. We should always try to react without anger because an angry person is prone to sinning, and that goes against God's Word.

Proverbs 29:11 - *"Fools give vent to their rage, but the wise bring calm in the end."* Only foolish people allow their rage to take over, unlike wise ones who keep their anger in check.

Proverbs 22:24 - *"Do not make friends with a hot tempered person; do not associate with one that is easily angered."* When we associate with people who have a bad temper, we can begin to behave like them. Just like a popular saying goes: "show me your friend, and I will tell you who you are."

James 4:1-2 - *"What causes quarrels and what causes fights among you? Is it not this, that your passions are at war within you? You desire and do not have, so you murder. You covet and cannot obtain, so you fight and quarrel. You do not have, because you do not ask."*

Anger and jealousy can make us misbehave, which can lead to sin. Instead of taking from others, ask God to provide you with what you need and to give you control over your anger.

The Bible admonishes us that holding on to anger can lead to sin, which is just one of the many reasons why letting go of anger is extremely important.

Additionally, letting go of anger clears our minds for more positive things in our lives, such as joy, happiness and gratitude. Whether one has a short temper or is easily upset about something that has been building up for some time, the above Bible references about anger will give us enough perspective and help us to decisively work through our anger.

There is a difference between healthy anger and smouldering or explosive anger that can do real damage to our lives, health, business, marital life, family, spirituality or education. Even those who hold exalted positions are not exempted, and it has no respect for gender or age.

Human beings are complex creatures, and our circumstances are therefore complex also. Our problems need to be understood in context and in perspective.

If all we knew of Noah was his problem with alcohol in Genesis 9, we would assume that he was a down-and-out loser. Yet, he was described by God as a *"just man, perfect in his generation"* (Genesis 6:9).

If all we knew of King David was his adultery with Bathsheba, we would never assume that he was, for the better part of his life, *"A man after God's heart"* (I Samuel 13:14).

Also, if all we knew about Saul of Tarsus was his efforts to kill Christ's followers, we would never expect him to become the Writer of half of the New Testament!

Moses was a man who lost his temper and better judgement at very critical moments during his lifetime. He seemed to have fought a battle with rage and anger throughout his entire life, a struggle he sometimes lost and sometimes won. Yet, in spite of his personal weakness, God used him to:

1. **Deliver His people from the bondage of slavery in Egypt**
2. **Lead the people of Israel to a new national identity**
3. **Establish the laws and structures of a brand new culture**
4. **Lead the Israelites to become a worshiping community, boldly committed to a God they had hitherto long forgotten**

Thus, by any standard of evaluation, Moses had an amazing track record, yet his weak point was anger, which dogged his steps throughout his entire life.

Peter struggled with impulsiveness; Solomon had wandering eyes for women, and Abraham had a manipulative spirit. Despite their weaknesses, Peter became a great fisher of men after he encountered Jesus Christ in Luke 5:1-7. Solomon wrote the very famous 31 chapters of the Book of Proverbs and was the wisest human on Earth, while his wealth and blessings cannot be rivalled, according to the Bible; Abraham, till today is still regarded as the father of faith, and the father of all Nations! We all must clearly identify any weakness that tries to ensnare us at any critical moment of our lives.

7

Is the Bible Very Categorial About Anger?

The ability to successfully handle anger is an important skill. Christian counsellors confirm that 50% of the people who come in for counselling have problems dealing with anger. As a counsellor, I can vividly testify to that postulation, especially based on what I wrote in the introductory part of this book. In case you have forgotten, I encourage you to revisit the opening pages of this book.

Anger can shatter communications, tear apart relationships, and could ruin both the joy and health of many. Sadly, however, people tend to always justify their anger instead of accepting responsibility for it. Everyone struggles in varying degrees with anger. But thankfully, God's Word contains principles regarding how to handle anger, as discussed earlier, and hereunder, in a godly manner, and how to overcome sinful anger!

Anger is not always seen by God, nor is it always seen in the Bible as a sin. There is a type of anger of which the Bible approves, often called "righteous indignation" God is angry (Psalm 7:11 & Mark 3:5), and it is acceptable to Believers to be very angry (Ephesians 4:26), which I had cited earlier.

Two Greek words in the New Testament are translated as "anger." One means "passion, energy," and the other means "agitated, boiling." Basically, anger is a God given energy which is intended to help us solve some of the problems we may face.

Examples of biblical anger include David's when he heard Nathan the Prophet sharing an injustice (2 Samuel 12) and Jesus' anger when some of the Jews had defiled worship at God's Temple in Jerusalem (John 2:13-18). We can see that neither of the two examples of anger involved any self defence but a defence of others or of a principle.

Having said that, it is important to recognize that anger at an injustice inflicted against oneself is also very appropriate. Anger has been said to be a "warning flag"- it alerts us to those times when others are usually attempting to or have violated our boundaries. God cares for every individual, but sadly, we do not always stand up for one another, meaning that sometimes we must stand up for ourselves! This is particularly important when considering the anger that victims usually feel.

Victims of abuse, violent crime or the like have been violated in some way; thus, often, while experiencing the trauma, they do not experience anger. Later, while working through the trauma, anger will eventually surface. And for a victim to reach a place of true health and forgiveness (which will be dealt with in the latter chapter of this book), he or she must first accept the trauma for what it was.

In order to fully accept that an act was unjust, one must sometimes experience anger. Because of the complexities of trauma recovery, this anger is often not short lived, especially for victims of abuse. Victims should process their anger and come to a place of acceptance and even forgiveness, which can often be a long journey. As God heals the victim, their emotions, including anger, will follow. Allowing the process to occur doesn't mean the person is living in sin; never. Anger can become sinful when it is motivated by pride (James 1:20), when it is quite unproductive and thus distorts God's purposes (I Corinthians 10:31), or when anger is allowed to linger (Ephesians 4:26-27).

One very obvious sign that anger has turned to sin is when, instead of attacking the problem at hand, we attack the wrongdoer. Ephesians 4:15-19 says we are to speak the truth in love and use our words to build others up, not allowing rotten or destructive words to pour from our lips. Unfortunately, this poisonous speech is a common characteristic of fallen men (Romans 3:13-14).

Anger becomes sin when it is allowed to boil over without restraint, resulting in a situation where hurt is multiplied (Proverbs 29:11), as discussed earlier, leaving devastation in its wake. Often, the consequences of uncontrollable anger are irreparable. Anger also becomes sin when the angry one refuses to be pacified, holds a grudge, or keeps it all inside (Ephesians 4: 26-27). This can cause depression and irritability over little things, which are often unrelated to the underlying problem.

We can obviously handle anger biblically by recognizing and admitting our prideful anger and/or our wrong handling of anger as sin (Proverbs 28:13 & I John 1:9). This confession should be both to God and to those who have been hurt by our anger. We should not minimize the sin by excusing it or by blame shifting. On the other hand, we can handle anger biblically by seeing God in the trial. This is especially important when people have done something too often to us. James 1:2-4, Romans 8:28-29, and Genesis 50:20 all point to the fact that God is sovereign over every circumstance.

Nothing happens to us that God does not allow or cause. Though God does allow bad things to happen, He is always faithful to redeem them for the good of His people because He is a good God (Psalm 145:8, 9 & 17). Reflecting on this truth until it moves from our head to our heart will alter how we react to those who hurt us. We can again handle anger biblically by making room for God's wrath. This is especially important in cases of "innocent" people. Genesis 50:49 and Romans 12:19 both tell us NOT to play God. God is righteous and just; we can trust Him who knows all and sees all to act justly (Genesis 18:25).

We can handle anger biblically by returning good for evil (Genesis 50:21 & Romans 12:21). This is key to converting our anger into love. Our actions can flow from our hearts, so also, our hearts can be altered by our actions (Matthew 5:43-48). That is, we can change our feelings towards another by changing how we choose to act toward that person.

We can handle anger biblically by communicating to solve the problem.

There are four basic rules of communication stated in Ephesians 4:15, 25-32, as shown hereunder:

1. **Be honest and speak:** Ephesians 4:15, 25 - People cannot read our minds. We must speak the truth with love.
2. **Stay current:** Ephesians 4:26-27 - We must not allow what is bothering us to build up until we lose control. It is important to deal with what is bothering us before it reaches a critical stage.
3. **Directly attack the problem, not the person:** Ephesians 4:29 & 31 -Along this line, we must remember the importance of keeping the volume of our voices low (Proverbs 15:1).
4. **Act, don't react:** Ephesians 4:31-32 - In view of our fallen nature, our first impulse is often a sinful one. The time spent in

"counting to ten" should be used to reflect upon the godly way to respond and to remind ourselves how the energy anger provided should be channelled to solve problems and NOT create bigger ones.

At times, we can handle anger preemptively by putting up stricter boundaries. We are told to be discerning (I Corinthians 2:15-16, Matthew 10:16). We need not "cast our pearls before swine" (Matthew 7:6). Meaning that sometimes our anger leads us to recognize that certain people are unsafe for us. While we can still forgive them, we may choose not to reenter the relationship.

Finally, we must intentionally work to solve our part of the problem, as encouraged in Romans 12:18. We cannot control how others act or respond, but we can make the changes that need to be made on our part. Overcoming ungodly anger is not accomplished overnight, but through constant prayers, Bible Studies and constant reliance upon the Holy Spirit, it can be overcome.

We may have allowed anger to become entrenched in our lives by habitual practice. Still, we can also practice responding correctly until that too becomes a habit and God is glorified in our response.

8

Forgiveness

Any book or write up that talks about the issue of "anger" are totally incomplete without including "forgiveness" as part of the main topics. That is why I decided to include this portion of the book as the closing chapter. I hope you have enjoyed the previous chapters.

It is instructive to mention that forgiveness is an integral aspect of our lives, generally. Although Jesus Christ emphasized forgiveness for believers, it cuts across almost all religions and beliefs, with the understanding that this is important if we want our hearts and lives to remain permanently unloaded and free.

We offend people, and people offend us. It is glaringly impossible to navigate throughout life without crossing each other's paths by offending one person or the other, whether deliberately or accidentally. Some people even continue to hold on to anger and grudges against people that have passed away. Of this, I am very certain because as an Apostle and a Guidance and Counselling Minister, I have heard and encountered numerous issues that relate to such on many occasions, within and outside my immediate place of abode!

A lot of people find it extremely difficult and, at times, even impossible to forgive those who have offended them. As believers, our Lord and Personal Saviour did not teach us to hold grudges till Eternity. He said we must always do everything that is humanly possible to forgive and that we must not allow sunset to "meet" grudges in our hearts, against whoever might have offended us. Not only that, when He was asked how many times someone could offend us before we can forgive the person, His answer was 70x7 times in a day for one offence or issue. The two references above are found in Ephesians 4:26 and Matthew 18:21-22, respectively.

Let us have an inept discussion about what the Bible says about this burning and very pertinent aspect of our lives.

Ephesians 4:32 - *"Be kind to one another, tenderhearted, forgiving one another, as God in Christ forgave you."*

Mark 11:25 - *"And whenever you stand praying, forgive, if you have anything against anyone, so that your Father also who is in heaven may forgive you your trespasses."*

I John 1:9 - *"If we confess our sins, He is faithful and just to forgive us our sins and to cleanse us from all unrighteousness."*

Matthew 6:15 - *"But if you do not forgive others their trespasses, neither will your Father forgive your trespasses."*

Matthew 18:21-22 - *"Then Peter came up and said to him, "Lord, how often will my brother sin against me, and I forgive him? As many as 7 times? Jesus said to him, "I do not say to you seven times, but seventy times seven."*

Matthew 6:14-15 - *"For if you forgive others their trespasses, your Father in heaven will also forgive you, but if you do not forgive others their trespasses, neither will your Father forgive your trespasses."*

Luke 6:37 - *"Judge not, and you will not be judged; condemn not and you will not be condemned; forgive, and you will be forgiven."*

Colossians 3:13 - *"Bearing with one another and if one complaints against another, forgiving each other; as the Lord has forgiven you, so you also must forgive."*

James 5:16 - *"Therefore, confess your sins to one another and pray for one another, that you may be healed. The prayer of a righteous person has great power as it is working."*

Romans 3:21-28 - *"But now the righteousness of God has been manifested apart from the law, although the Law and the Prophets bear witness to it - the righteousness of God through faith in Jesus Christ for all who believe. For there is no distinction: for all have sinned and fall short of the glory of God; and are justified by His Grace as a gift, through the redemption that is in Christ Jesus, whom God put forward as a propitiation by His Blood, to be received by faith. This was to show God's righteousness because He had passed over former sins."*

Luke 17:3 - *"Pay attention to yourself! If your brother sins, rebuke him, and if he repents, forgive him."*

I Peter 4:8 - *"Above all, keep loving one another earnestly, since love covers a multitude of sins."*

Psalm 130:3 - *"If you, O Lord should mark iniquities, O Lord, who could stand?"*

Matthew 6:12-15 - *"And forgive us our debts, as we also have forgiven our debtors. And lead us not into temptation, but deliver us from evil. For if you forgive others their trespasses, your Heavenly Father will also forgive you, but if you do not forgive others their trespasses, neither will your Father forgive your trespasses."*

Matthew 18: 33-35 - *"And should not you have had mercy on your fellow servant, as I had mercy on you? And in anger his master delivered him to the jailers, until he should pay all his debt. So also my Heavenly Father will do to every one of you, if you do not forgive your brothers from your heart."*

Proverbs 28:9 - *"If one turns away his ear from hearing the law even his prayer is an abomination."*

Galatians 6:1 - *"Brothers, if anyone is caught in any transgression, you who are spiritual should restore him in a spirit of gentleness. Keep watch on yourself, lest you too be tempted."*

Psalm 38: 3-4 - *"There is no soundness in my flesh because of your indignation; there is no health in my bones because of my sin. For my iniquities have gone over my head; like a heavy burden, they are too heavy for me."*

2 Chronicles 30:9 - *"For if you return to the Lord, your brother and your Children will find compassion with their captors and return to this land. For the Lord you God is gracious and merciful and will not turn away His face from you, if you return to Him."*

Jeremiah 3:12 - *"Go, and proclaim these words toward the North, and say, "Return, faithless Israel, declares the Lord. I will not look on you in anger, for I am merciful, declares the Lord; I will not be angry forever."*

I Peter 3:9 - *"Do not repay evil for evil or reviling for reviling, but on the contrary, bless, for to this you were called, that you may obtain a blessing."*

Colossians 3:12-13 - *"Put on then, as God's chosen Ones, holy and beloved, compassionate hearts, kindness, humility, meekness and patience, bearing with one another and if one has a complaint against another, forgiving each other, as the Lord has forgiven you, so you also must forgive."*

Joel 2:13 - *"and rend your hearts and not your garments, "Return to the Lord your God, for He is gracious and merciful, slow to anger, and abounding in steadfast love; and He relents over disaster."*

Matthew 6:9-15 - *"Pray then like this:"Our Father in heaven, hallowed be your Name. Your Kingdom come, your will be done, on Earth as it is in heaven. Give us this day, our daily bread and forgive us our debts, as we also have forgiven our debtors. And lead us not into temptation......Amen."*

Ephesians 4:31 - *"Let all bitterness and wrath and anger and clamour and slander be put away from you, along with all malice."*

Others are Matthew 7:21-23, Matthew 18:23-35, Galatians 5:22, Micah 7:18-20, I Kings 8: 46-48, James 2:8, Proverbs 15:1, 2 Corinthians 2:5-11, I John 2:2, Psalm 51:2-5, Matthew 18:21-35, John 8:7, James 5:14-15, Hebrews 8:12, Isaiah 43:25-26, Acts 7:59-60, Luke 23:33-34, Jeremiah 31:34, Hebrews 10:17, Colossians 1:13-14, John 13:34, 2 Chronicles 7:14, and Proverbs 15:21.

The following are equally very relevant: Luke 7:44-50, I John 1:9-10, Psalm 103:12, Romans 12:20, Isaiah 55:7, Ecclesiastes 7:20, Daniel 9:9, Proverbs 28:13, Psalm 32:5, Isaiah 1:18, Romans 3:23, Proverbs 17:9, Luke 6:27, James 5:16, and John 3:16.

A cursory look into all, any or a combination of any of the above Golden verses would confirm that we have all been in situations where we have done wrong and desire forgiveness, either from a spouse, family member, friend, or even a co-worker. Sometimes the person we need forgiveness from the most is ourselves. And then there are the times when someone asks us for forgiveness, and we have to look deeply within ourselves to offer it with no strings attached. It is usually hard, but we just have to let go and forget totally. Thus, whether you are giving or receiving forgiveness, it is a very powerful thing, and you must cultivate the habit of doing so wholeheartedly, without any reservations.

In addition to what the scriptures teach us and encourage us to do about anger and forgiveness, there are other physical angles to it. Until the rift between two parties (human beings or individuals) has been amicably settled, a lot of psychological factors would continue to unavoidably dominate the lives of those that are involved or concerned. Once they see the other party, either from a close or a long distance, a sort of fury or negative feeling or reaction can automatically erupt from their hearts. Heartbeats of either party begin to palpitate swiftly, simply because the eyes have seen " a perceived enemy." This could continue to play out even without seeing each other but by mere mentioning, remembering or hearing the name of either of the parties. It would easily ring a bell in the ears that "one's perceived enemy" is still alive. Ill feelings or bad thoughts would begin to move within the person's mind, and it could be extremely dangerous for the stability or the person's health. Such could lead to depression, hypertension, insomnia, sickness or even shortage of breath. The overall or ultimate effect could be an untimely death if someone has such issues with many people without resolving them as soon as practical! That is why, apart from attempting to block or debar our prayers from being answered by God, keeping malice and refusing to be at peace with everybody (though it may not be practically possible) must be avoided. The Bible clearly enjoins us to strive to do so; it goes a very long way to enhance our wellness, well-being and overall welfare.

9

The Role of Love

Having given wide attention to the issue of anger and forgiveness from the foregoing, it is very apt and pertinent to attempt to round up the writing of this book by delving into the role of love in all that we have discussed.

A lot of people find it very difficult to forgive each other, although Jesus Christ enjoins us to love and forgive each other, as pointed out in the above chapters. If we genuinely love each other as ourselves and can constantly bear it in mind that no human being is perfect, it behooves us to always ensure that we should quickly forgive ourselves and put all issues of rancour, malice, quarrels and sharp disagreements behind us.

Love is one thing that unites all of human existence. It has the ability to inspire, encourage and lighten our hearts. If genuinely practiced, it can be the greatest feeling in the world; but it can also be confusing. In times when love is hard to understand, we need wisdom or reassurance. The word of God is the perfect resource to turn to, as it holds the best representation of love. The Bible is the best succour and shelter for the confused heart.

The Scriptures have a lot to say about love. The Bible encourages us to practice love genuinely wherever we find ourselves - between spouses, among friends, within the family, with our co-workers, among Lovers and among our Neighbours. Doing so would reduce tension everywhere; we would be our brothers' keeper at all times; we would be able to move freely once we are sure and convinced that nobody would be looking for our downfall, and progress would continue to grow and radiate within and around us.

Below are some Golden Verses to support the issue of love, which equally encourage us to avoid anger and embrace forgiveness.

Genesis 2:24 - *"Therefore a man shall leave his father and his mother and hold fast to his wife, and they shall become one flesh."*

I Corinthians 16:14 - *"Do everything in love."*

Ephesians 5:25 - *"For husbands, this means love your wives, just as Christ loved the Church. He gave up His life for her."*

Romans 13:8 - *"Owe no one anything except to love each other; for the one who loves another has fulfilled the law."*

Colossians 3:14 - *"And over all these virtues put on love, which binds them all together in perfect unity."*

I John 2:9-10 - *"Anyone who claims to be in the light but hates a brother or sister is still in the darkness. Anyone who loves their brother and sister lives in the light, and there is nothing in them to make them stumble."*

I John 4:8 - *"Whoever does not love does not know God, because God is love."*

Romans 12:9-10 - *"Love must be sincere. Hate what is evil; cling to what is good. Be devoted to one another in love. Honour one another above yourselves."*

I Corinthians 13:4-5 - *"Love is patient, love is kind. It doesn't envy, it does not boast, it is not proud. It does not dishonour others; it is not self-seeking, it is not easily angered, it keeps no record of wrongs."*

Proverbs 3:3-4 - *"Let love and faithfulness never leave you. Bind them around your neck, write them on the tablet of your heart. Then you will win favour and a good name in the sight of God and man."*

I Peter 4:8 - *"Above all, love each other deeply because love covers over a multitude of sins."*

Proverbs 10:12 - *"Hatred stirs up conflict, but love covers over all wrongs."*

I Corinthians 13:6-7 - *"Love does not delight in evil but rejoices with the truth. It always protects, always trusts, always hopes, always perseveres."*

I John 4:7 - *"Beloved, let us love one another, for love is from God, and whoever loves has been born of God, and knows God."*

I John 4:9-11 - *"This is how God showed His love among us: He sent His One and only Son into the world that we might live through Him. This is love; not that we loved God, but that He loved us and send His Son as an atoning sacrifice for our sins. Dear friends, since God so loved us, we also ought to love one another."*

I Corinthians 13:13 - *"And now abideth faith, hope, love, these three but the greatest of these is love."*

Finally, and in conclusion, we must do everything that is humanly possible to avoid anger. Try to be at peace with everybody because the Bible enjoins us to do so according to Romans 12:18, thus, *"If it is possible, as much as lieth in you, live peaceably with all men."*

As I mentioned in the introductory part of this book, anger is a very dangerous aspect of our lives, especially if it has to do with negative anger. Let me emphasize that it comes with verbal abuse, cursing, negative tendencies and the application of unprintable words. Such words could continue to linger in the minds or hearts of both the speaker and the listener, and if care is not taken, forgiveness could become extremely impossible. But as elaborately explained, no matter the tension that might have been created hitherto, amicable settlement and resolution must be brokered at all costs.

Anger could even pave the way for a permanent disability such as breaking of limbs, injuries sustained during the exchange of aggravating hot words in the period the anger was becoming seriously charged, and temperamental emotions which become totally uncontrollable. We must thus constantly remember what the Bible says in Proverbs 18:21, *"Death and life are in the power of the tongue, and they that love it shall eat the fruit thereof."*

Another major aspect of the Bible that I would love to recommend for our regular reference is the Book of James, Chapter 3. There are many portions of the Bible that greatly encourage us to always be on guard with what we say under any negative provocation, but this particular Chapter of the Book of James and Romans Chapter 12 are hereunder reproduced verbatim in order to make it handy for us, at all times.

Thus, Romans 12:1-21 says, *"I beseech thee….. but overcome evil with good."* On the other hand, James 3:1-18 goes thus, *"My Brethren, be not many masters, knowing that…… and the fruit of righteousness is sown in peace of them that make peace."*

My final advice? Endeavour to buy as many copies of this book as possible and give them as special presents to any of your loved ones who have been struggling with how to permanently avoid or totally overcome negative anger or who easily become temperamentally emotional. They will forever remember and appreciate you as long as they live.

God bless you.

A Sinner's Prayer

Dear Heavenly Father,

I come to You in the Name of Jesus Christ.

You said in Your Word, "Whosoever shall call upon the name of the Lord shall be saved" (Romans 10:13). I am calling on Your Name, so I know You have saved me now.

You also said that "if you confess with your mouth the Lord Jesus and believe in your heart that God has raised Him from the dead, you will be saved. For with the heart one believes unto righteousness, and with the mouth, confession is made unto salvation" (Romans 10:9-10). I believe in my heart Jesus Christ is the Son of God. I believe that He was raised from the dead for my justification, and I confess Him now as my Lord and Savior.

Thank you, Lord, because now, I am saved!

Thank You, Lord, because I know you have heard my prayer. Thank You, Lord, because I am now born again.

Signed _____

Date _____

About the Author

Apostle Dr. Victor Adekunle Adewusi was a passionate Spiritual Leader and Father of many children and grandchildren.

He was also the Author of five books *"The Secrets of Happy Parenting," "Control Your Anger," "Praise, Appreciation & Thanksgiving (PAT)," "Mine Shall Be Done,"* and *"Fear Not, Cheer Up, Do Not Despair."*

Until his passing, he was the General Overseer of The Eternal Sacred Order of The Cherubim and Seraphim Church, Oke Ibukun Branco; The Governor of the Yabatech Class of 1986 governing council; a Member of The Chartered Institute of Management; A Fellow of The Chartered Institute of Taxation of Nigeria and A Fellow of The Institute of Chartered Accountants of Nigeria (ICAN).

Apostle Dr. Victor Adekunle, who was a philanthropist, has drawn on his personal breakthrough life experiences to help people overcome challenges and attain greater achievements in their life.

www.ingramcontent.com/pod-product-compliance
Lightning Source LLC
Chambersburg PA
CBHW070342010526
44107CB00004B/593